From Puppy to Service Dog

The PTSD Service Dog

From Puppy to Service Dog

The PTSD Service Dog

Lu Barrett

Dogs&Jobs

The PTSD Service Dog Copyright © 2017 by Dogs&Jobs.

www.dogsandjobs.com

Book and Cover design by Yes!Design

ISBN: 978-1-945895-03-6

First Edition: December 2017

For all the men and women who were still children when they had to experience the unimaginable.

CONTENTS

CHAPTER 1 1

CHAPTER 2 3

CHAPTER 3 11

CHAPTER 4 15

CHAPTER 5 17

CHAPTER 6 19

CHAPTER 7 20

ABOUT THE AUTHOR 73

Foreword

I assume that you hold this book in your hands because you wonder if a PTSD service dog can help you. Unfortunately, I can't relieve you of your pain or undo the terrible anguish you suffered. However, I do hope that through this book you learn how a PTSD service dog can help you. Maybe with this book I can give you a small hope that someday your day-to-day life can become a bit easier.

When I began with the training of PTSD service dogs, this type of service dog was still entirely unknown in Europe. Even then, years ago, it was my desire to one day help as many affected people as possible. If I'm able to help some of you by sharing my knowledge in this book, I have already reached that goal.

You, moreso than most, have a right to finally be happy and live a life without fear and suffering.

I wish you much joy while reading this book, and wish you to one day be alright – with or without a service dog.

CHAPTER 1

The PTSD Service Dog

Oftentimes, dogs are better than people. Their mere presence can help others recover some amount of joy in life. As a best friend, thousands of dogs give comfort to ill people everyday. While therapy dogs help in doctor's offices and clinics, PTSD service dogs can do so much more. They are neither companion dogs nor therapy dogs. PTSD service dogs give hope for the future. They are specially selected and trained many months for their job, which is to actively alleviate the stress from those suffering with post-traumatic stress disorder. These special canines reduce limitations in everyday life and encourage a life worth looking forward to. When you don't leave your apartment for weeks out of fear, the PTSD service dog will give you security outside of your home, and can also keep people at a distance when you need. Do you know the feeling when you stand in the grocery store and are overcome by a paralyzing panic? You want to run, but suddenly you don't know where to go, or even how to leave. The PTSD service dog has learned to guide you to the exit or to a quiet place until you feel better. Is your everyday life dominated by flashbacks, dissociations and nightmares? The PTSD service dog can interrupt these scary scenarios while comforting you. With a PTSD service dog, you are never alone. They accompany you 24 hours a day, seven days a week. They are always happy to be by your side, regardless of whether you are having a good or a bad day.

CHAPTER 2

Which disorders are suitable for a PTSD service dog?

PTSD service dogs, like mobility service dogs, guide dogs and seizure alert dogs, belong to the category of service dogs. PTSD service dogs are specially trained to help overcome the complex limitations of a post-traumatic stress disorder, including the entire spectrum of dissociative disorders. Additionally, there are other service dogs for different psychological and psychiatric disorders, as well as eating disorders, severe depression, bipolar disorder and schizophrenia.

What is PTSD?

PTSD means post-traumatic stress disorder, and it is the result of a single traumatic experience, or multiple ones. Unlike simple PTSD, complex PTSD is caused by severe and continous traumatizations. The effects of complex PTSD extends to all aspects of life and has long-lasting effects. Complex PTSD can manifest itself in the form of dissociative disorders, amnesia, depression symptoms, fear, panic attacks, self-destructive behavior, suicidal thoughts, chronic guilt, low self-esteem, psychosomatic afflictions, social withdrawal, problems with proximity, and hypervigilance. The symptoms can oftentimes be alleviated through therapy. However, in most cases, the effects of severe complex traumas can not be completely cured, leaving the afflicted person to suffer for life.

Can a PTSD service dog cure my affliction?

No, the PTSD service dog can only learn to react to your commands, thereby helping you to better manage your everyday life.

When combined with psychotherapy, a PTSD service dog can help you reclaim your life. Additionally you should be willing to accept and react to your dog's help.

The PTSD service dog can sometimes even help you directly. For example, by keeping others at a distance, or making you become aware of a behavior. If you have discussed this behavior with your therapist, the dog can encourage you to adjust to a more positive behavior while in the moment.

I have witnessed many small wonders in my years training PTSD service dogs:

A woman who hadn't left her home in years found the courage to leave her house daily through the service dog.

Another woman who could not break contact with her perpetrators managed to do so with the help of her PTSD service dog. Here, the dog peacefully intervened and would not let her tormentors near.

For each of these women, life has gotten better with a PTSD service dog. They feel safer. However, a dog does not make all symptoms completely disappear. The PTSD service dog is always just additional support for other therapy options.

Is a PTSD service dog right for me?

You will find the answer to this question in your heart. Take your time when finding out if a PTSD service dog can help you. Consider all aspects, and decide in the end if you are ready for a PTSD service dog. In case you come to the conclusion that it is not the right time for a dog, keep it in the back of your mind as a possibility for later. Maybe the right time will be in two or three years, or maybe it will never be.

Use the following table to determine if now is the the right time for a PTSD service dog:

- ✓ Do I suffer from a complex PTSD and have I already completed psychotherapy, or am I currently under treatment?
- ✓ Do I suffer from the symptoms to a degree that everyday life is impossible?
- ✓ Do I personally believe that a PTSD service dog can improve my quality of life?
- ✓ Do I personally believe that a psychotherapy alone won't help as much as having a PTSD service dog for additional support?
- ✓ Do I like dogs?
- ✓ Am I walking the dog at least three times a day and enabling socialization with other dogs?

- ✓ Do I want a dog around me 24 hours a day, a dog that I can never take a break from?
- ✓ Even if I am unwell and would rather just stay in bed, will I, for the dog's sake, get out of bed, feed, and walk the dog?
- ✓ Do I want to commit to bonding with a dog for many years?
- ✓ Can I handle the fact that the dog will die some day?
- ✓ Am I ready to take responsibility for another living being, even if that means that I have to limit self-destructive or suicidal tendencies for the animal's sake?
- ✓ Am I able to give a dog the attention, affection, food and water that they need?
- ✓ Am I prepared to train a puppy right from the start?
- ✓ Do I have the patience to forgive a puppy's mistakes?
- ✓ If the dog makes a mistake, will I be ready to question what I might have done wrong to cause his behavior, instead of automatically blaming the dog?
- ✓ Am I willing to take the dog everywhere with me, even on vacation?
- ✓ Am I strong enough to deal with other people if they don't want to let my dog into their store?
- ✓ Am I ready to invest additional time and energy to train the dog?
- ✓ Did I previously have a bad experience with a dog that could influence my behavior towards him in a negative way?
- ✓ If something happens to me, do I have the support of friends or a therapist so that the dog will be taken care of?

Even if you have no loved ones, it should not stop you from getting the help of a PTSD service dog. Many service dog owners are alone. There are always solutions! A couple of years ago, I set up an emergency hotline with a center for service dogs for exactly this purpose. After an incoming call to the emergency hotline, which is available at all times, a temporary replacement trainer will immediately drive to the dog and take care of him until the owner is able to do it himself again.

Consider all of these aspects. If the positives outweigh the negatives, and you are ready to accept the conditions, then I wish for you to have a four-pawed helper by your side very soon.

Am I fit for a PTSD service dog?

Most people that I help have asked themselves this very question from time to time. Most of them add that they are worried that the dog might be unhappy by their side. I can relieve you of this fear! If you love your PTSD service dog, play with them, train them and walk them multiple times a day, feed them, care for them, enable them to play with other dogs, and never mistreat them, then they will surely be happy. A dog does not judge you. Your dog doesn't care about how you look today or what you have been through. They love you unconditionally! Your dog will never be deterred simply because you spend the better part of three weeks in your bed due to a crisis. In fact, they will lay down next to you to warm you. Do not forget: you are this creature's life! They don't know any other lifestyle, and will be appreciative of everything you give them so long as it is always done with a loving heart and is in their best interests.

If you are worried that you might forget your dog's feeding times or walks due to dissociation or amnesia, here is a little trick: hang notes inside of your home that say things like, "walk with the dog at 9" or "feed the dog at 12". Be sure to check off every point immediately after you fulfil each task.

In case you have a dissociative identity disorder, you should communicate with every inner person so that everyone accepts the plan and reliably checks off a point once it is done.

No dog on this planet needs expensive beds, bowls of gold, or a big house. A dog will be happy if they can be with their human. A dog can be happy in the smallest hut or a one-room apartment. This is what a PTSD service dog can do – be by your side at all times!

I know no one with PTSD that didn't at least once say something like, "My dog would be better off somewhere else." If you are ever feeling the same way, please remember that it's normal to feel this way from time to time, and most people experience this. However, these things are not related to the dog, but are instead closely linked to the feelings of inadequacy.

I assure you, if you did not harm your dog, and you gave them enough food and water, and let them outside to do their business, then there is no person your dog would rather be with than you!

Most service dogs couldn't live without their human and would be unhappy anywhere without him. For your service dog, your life is completely ordinary. As a species, your dog has no idea that people usually don't panic when the telephone or the doorbell rings. Your dog loves and accepts you the way you are, because it is the life that they are used to and desire. Who else could play with them and be silly? Who could train like you? Service dogs usually have a way stronger connection to their owner than other dogs. You live close with each other, are always there for each other and help each other.

CHAPTER 3

Is every dog suitable?

Once you have decided that a dog can help you merely through his presence, and that he doesn't have to perform certain tasks, then any dog that you can commit yourself to is suitable. If, however, you want a real service dog who can help you in public situations by performing specific tasks, then the dog has to have certain abilities.

What if I already have a dog?

Theoretically, you can evaluate whether or not your current dog has the necessary abilities to be a PTSD service dog. If so, you can train your dog to perform required tasks to make them a PTSD service dog.

Unfortunately, in most cases your dog won't be suitable, either because they are too anxious, or they are not compatible with every other dog. Even so, a companion dog can still be a strong and effective support.

What to do about other pets?

A lot of people already have cats or other small animals before they get a PTSD service dog. If you adopt a grown dog, you should make sure he is used to cats or other small animals. Normally, it should not be a problem with puppies, because all puppies are able to get accustomed to other pets.

The Nature of the PTSD Service Dog

Compared to other service dogs, you should make sure that the PTSD service dog has a particularly good temperament. They should not show any anxieties, insecurities or aggressions whatsoever, and they should not be too sensitive, either. If they were too sensitive, they would be unsettled by you feeling sad or experiencing a panic attack, and they would not be able to effectively help.

If you're looking for a dog who would seriously protect you, you should know that a service dog could never do that. Every service dog has to be friendly at any given time.

If protection is your main priority, you should think about whether a real protection dog would be more appropriate than a service dog. For protection purposes, a Bullmastiff, Presa Carnario, German Shepherd and Malinois would be more suitable.

One book in particular best describes how you can find an appropriate PTSD service dog, called *From Puppy to Service Dog – Selection, Standards, Training.*

The Size of the PTSD Service Dog

For the choice of an appropriate PTSD service dog, you should always make sure which kind of tasks they can fulfil later on. If you want the dog to create distance between you and other people, then they should measure at least 20 inches. Also, as far as deterring conflict goes, the bark of a Chihuahua hasn't got the same impact as a German Shepherd. In the end, it is your decision which dog suits you best.

CHAPTER 4

How to Get a PTSD Service Dog

There are several ways to get a PTSD service dog. You can train your own dog with or without a trainer's assistance.

If you feel unable to train a puppy to be public-access-ready, you can obtain a fully trained service dog from a program or private trainer.

If you receive SSDI or SSI, you can apply for a PTSD service dog at a non-profit organization. Those organizations usually donate fully trained service dogs to those who qualify.

If you get SSDI or SSI, you can also try to get financial support for the training of a PTSD service dog with a service dog trainer via donations or foundations.

Considering the costs, you have to keep in mind that you also have to pay for the purchase and the living of the dog. You should put aside some money every month or take out health insurance for your puppy, just in case he becomes unexpectedly sick.

CHAPTER 5

Managing a Service Dog's Stress

I am often asked if a PTSD service dog can be exposed to too much stress, and if I can expect them to cope with every type of PTSD. First, you can best prevent overwhelming your dog with stress by choosing a dog with a stable temperament, the kind of dog will not be upset if you cry, rampage or shout. Nevertheless, the dog may get stressed by you not reacting to a signal. For example, attempts to interrupt your dissociations.

Your dog wants to do everything right and hopes to interrupt the dissociation and get praised by you. If this does not happen, he might feel alienated. Some dogs try to fulfil the task again while others withdraw and show signs of stress. To the benefit of your dog, you should make an effort to improve yourself and quickly react positively to his actions, and to always praise him.

You should also try hard, not to transfer your anxieties to

your puppy. Talk to your therapist about how to behave if you feel anxious in crowds so as to not let your dog feel these anxieties during the necessary socialisation process.

If you consider these aspects at all times, then your service dog shouldn't feel a lot of stress.

CHAPTER 6

The History of PTSD Service Dogs

PTSD service dogs are quite a new kind of service dog. PTSD service dogs borrow elements from other kinds of service dogs, like guide dogs.

The first PTSD service dogs were trained by an affected person in the U.S. in 1997. In 2002, the Psychiatric Service Dog Society, a grassroot organization, formed to enlighten the public about service dogs for mental and psychiatric conditions, and to offer help with the training. For years, PTSD service dogs were owner trained by the affected people themselves. When soldiers came back with a PTSD from Afghanistan and Iraq in 2008, service dog organizations in the U.S. started training PTSD service dogs for veterans.

CHAPTER 7

The Tasks

When you start training your dog, always keep in mind that there is no time frame for your dog to perform certain tasks. If you're feeling unwell for a few weeks or months, you can reduce your dog's training.

Don't get stressed. Choose your own pace to train.

Before starting with the special PTSD tasks, your dog should already know basic obedience and standards, as described in the book *From Puppy to Service Dog – Selection, Standards, Training*. On this account, the training of the PTSD tasks mostly starts between the age of 12 and 18 months.

There is a long list of tasks for PTSD service dogs to learn. Normally, dogs only learn three to five of these tasks. Which of the tasks a PTSD service dog learns depends on the individual requirements of the owner.

Look at the list of PTSD service dogs tasks and decide which are helpful for you. Take a pen and a piece of paper while you read the tasks and write down the names of the tasks that are considered. In doing so, you can begin to generate a training schedule and decide exactly which tasks your dog has to learn.

The tasks for post-traumatic stress disorder (PTSD) service dogs are divided in two categories:

I.   *External tasks:* these commands are followed by the dog, and can be recognized by any person.

II.   *Processing tasks:* these commands are not as easily recognizable by the general public. Among these tasks are:

   ❖ *Cognitive behavior tasks:* this combines the in-therapy techniques learned by the patient with special cues from the dog. A dog's task alerts the patient to question a certain behavior or patterns of thoughts.

   ❖ *Natural behavior tasks:* these are techniques that follow canine instinct and come easily to service dogs. For example, the dog uses a special reality check to indicate there is someone in a room who scares the patient. In case nobody is in the room, the dog will remain calm, but if there is somebody in the room, the dog will become curious and greet him or her.

   ❖ *Regulating behavior:* this is where the dog alerts the patient to a certain behavior by using an trained command. The patient can then use techniques learned in therapy to stop this behavior. In case the dog points out a flashback, the patient uses the appropriate techniques to control it.

Turn on the light in dark rooms (external task)

The dog is able to turn on the lights when the two of you first come home. All you need for this task is a Post-It or a target stick. I will explain the exercise with the Post-It, but using the target stick works in the same way.

Stick the Post-It onto your hand and hold it close to your dog. Make sure to choose a color different from your skin. For example, blue. Since dogs are unable to differentiate between a lot of colors, the dog might recognize colors such as red, yellow, green and brown as skin color. Each time the dog becomes interest in the Post-It note or object you are targetting with your stick, reward him with a click and a treat. Afterwards, only reward him when the nose touches the Post-It.

Introduce the appropriate command by saying, "good boy (or girl). Touch!" Use the click first, then the treat. After a few repeats, you should start training the dog by giving the command "Touch" first, meaning you show the dog the Post-It, say "touch", and then the dog touches the Post-It. Once the dog is following your command correctly, you may continue the training with the next step. Stick the Post-It onto a lightswitch, and give your dog "touch" command. If your dog doesn't touch the lightswitch right away, you are allowed to give a little help by pointing out the lightswitch while giving the command. After a few repeats, give your dog the new command "Good boy (or girl). Touch light!" Make sure to only reward your dog if he touches the switch, not the wall. When your dog is confident touching the switch, start ripping the Post-It into small pieces until there is only a tiny shred left on the switch when you give the command "Light". Eventually, your dog will touch the switch when given the command "Light", even though there is no Post-It left. Start increasing the distance between you and the light switch until you are able to stand at the entrance door and give your dog the command "Light". Make sure to start training with different light switches and introduce distractions.

You should make this command standard practice every time the two of you come home.

Open the door (external task)

The dog is able to open doors and get your mobile phone, medication or emergency phone. In order to do this task, your dog needs to be familiar with the commands "pull" and "Go back" (as described in the book *From Puppy to Service Dog - Selection, Standards, Trainings.*)

This task consists of a chain series of actions. When your dog pulls confidentially on a cloth, you can tie it up on the first-third of the door-handle (make sure to secure it carefully, it needs to stay in place even if the dog pulls). To ensure that the dog experiences a success, you can decide to leave the door a little open at the beginning.

Start the training by going to the door with your dog and give him the command "pull". Once your dog pulls at the door, give him the command "go back". When the door moves, reward your dog with a click and a treat. In the next step, you'll give your dog both commands at the same time ("pull and go back") so that your dog does both actions at once. In case your dog doesn't want to pull on the cloth, you should reward every interest the dog shows in the cloth with a click and a treat.

Repeat the "pull" command and open the door a few times, and then, after the click add the new order "Good boy (or girl). Open the door!". Once your dog understands what "Open the door" means, you can replace "Pull and go back" with "Open the door", and start giving the command first.

As soon as your dog opens the door when you give him the command, you may close the door. Your dog needs to gain more strength to open the door. Keep motivating your dog if he wants to give up because of the door's resistance. Once your dog is successful, reward him with a click and a treat.

For the final step, you'll need a extra person to help you. The purpose of this step is to teach your dog to go out of the door after opening it instead of immediately walking up to you for a treat.

At first, the other person should stand 40 to 78 inches behind the closed door.

Give your dog the command "Open the door", but do not reward once the door opens. Instead, the other person needs to call the dog to come. Once the dog approaches the other person, you may reward him. Gradually increase the distance of the person and the door, and eventually out of your home by not calling the dog every time he opens the door. After trying this a few times, your dog should go out of the door automatically after open it.

Getting Medication (external task)

Your dog retrieves your medication.

For this task, you should keep your medication in a box that your dog can carry. A plastic box can be used or even a lunchbox. To ensure your dog can find the box at any time, you should always put the box back in the same spot. For instance, you can choose your coffee table or your kitchen counter. If the pills are in a drawer, your dog can learn first to open the drawer the same way as the "open door" command.

Concerning fetching, it is important that objects are not damaged, and that the dog learns not to run after flying objects. Therefore, you should not just throw the box in front of your dog, but instead train solid fetching skills.

Hold your palm to your dog. At every show of interest in your palm, click and reward. If the dog touches your palm, you click and reward the dog by saying "thanks".

Now, practice gently handing over an object. Give a toy to your dog. If your dog has been trained by the clicker, they will normally give you whatever they have in order to get the treat as soon as they hear the clicking noise. When your dog drops the toy, hold your hand under the toy and click while saying "thanks".

If your dog nudges your hand reliably on the command "thanks", you can go one step further: Hold the box in front of your dog and waggle it. You positively reinforce every interest, from sniffling to taking into the mouth. If the dog takes it into the mouth you click and say "take meds". If he puts it in your hand you say "thanks".

Slowly prolong the duration of time that the dog keeps the box in his mouth before clicking, and before giving the box to you. You practice that step until your dog reliably picks up the box on "take" and carries it until you command "thanks", even if the dog has to make circles around you or has to carry the box in his mouth through the whole apartment. While carrying it, you can praise your dog now by saying "get meds".

Then, you put the box to a certain spot and show your dog where you have placed it. You stand next to your dog and command "take meds". If he picks it up when you are not holding the box, you click. If he gives it to you, you say "thanks". If he is not able to immediately pick it up because it is harder to grasp, help him at first by putting the box's corner on an edge so that he can grab it from a better angle. Next, repeat these steps until you have reached another room. Your dog has to get you the box now on the command "take meds" from a greater distance. If your dog gets the box reliably, you can say "get medicine" after the box is in his mouth. As he approaches you, confirm as before. In the later stages, you don't say "take meds" and "get meds" anymore, but simply "get medicine" for all two steps.

Medication Reminders (external task and regulating behavior)

Your dog reminds you to take your medication.

This task goes with the task of getting medication. Surely, you are wondering how your dog is supposed to know when you have to take your medication. Your dog can't know that you have to take your medication at a certain time, so you should combine your dosage time with a particular activity. If you have to take your medication after getting up in the morning, you should set an alarm clock. If the alarm clock rings, you command "get meds". If the dog gets you the medication upon the ring, click, praise and reward. You can also practice this lesson during the day by getting into bed and setting the alarm clock. Then you command your dog to "get meds" after the alarm clock rings. After 400 to 1,000 repetitions, your dog will link the sound of the alarm clock with getting the medication, and he will always run to get the medication once he hears the alarm clock. Consistency is important – let your dog get the medication after every alarm, even if you don't need them in that moment.

If you take your medication at noon, after lunch, command "get meds" right after having eaten, and while still at the table.

Alternatively, you can also set your alarm at a certain time, so that your dog will get the medication on hearing the alarm.

Look Out

Door Security

Indicating People Approaching from Behind

Emergency Phone

Interrupting Flashbacks

How to create Distance

Go to the Car

Getting Water (external task and regulating behavior)

Here, your dog gets you water as a reminder to take your medication.

You should combine this task with the task of getting medication. If your dog brings your medication, you immediately say "get water". For this task, a water bottle should be placed at the same spot every time (just like the box).

Plastic bottles – 16oz each – are especially suitable. Practice fetching the bottle just like you did with fetching the box. You can let your dog fetch an empty bottle in the beginning, then you fill the bottle a quarter full, then fill halfway, and then fill three quarters, until your dog is able to fetch a full bottle of water.

Getting Cell Phones (external task)

Your dog gets you your cell phone so that you can call support during a crisis. Practice fetching the cell phone just like getting the box until your dog reliably gets you the cell phone on the command, "get phone".

If you worry about your cell phone, you can firstly practice fetching with an old phone.

Emergency Phone
(external task)

Your dog calls for help via emergency phone, if you are unconscious.

If you suffer from suicidal thoughts or from strong side effects of medication, ask for this task. The most frequent sentence I have heard concerning this topic is, "I know these medical alert systems are offered by Alert1 or Philips Lifeline." While the latter statement is correct, the emergency phone does not extend to medical alert systems. Concerning these medical alert systems, you normally have to pay a monthly fee, and the staff of the service provider will be alerted. The emergency phone represents a one-time purchase under 100 Dollars, which substitutes a landline telephone and notifies relatives. Maybe you have heard of senior citizen phones with emergency call buttons? They have emergency transmitters, but they are too small for a dog's paw. As a result, we limit ourselves to an SOS button, but even that is still too small for many dogs. However, you can modify the SOS button by dividing a cork gluing a small piece to the SOS button. Use a coloured chip to the cork. For instance, a chip from a poker game.

If your dog pushes that SOS button, there is a loud alarm for 15 seconds. This alarm makes it possible to help people in the apartment, or to stop the emergency call in case of a false alarm. After the alarm, some emergency phones automatically calls 10 or 20 pre-set phone numbers in rapid succession. Most people save the phone number of the therapist, friends, or the service dog's trainer. Even if it seems logical to save 911 first, you should clarify that with the 911 staff responsible for your region in advance.

Before putting the phone into operation, you should record a message that can be heard by the called person if the emergency call is triggered. For example: "Merle, my service dog, just activated this emergency call because I am lying unconscious in my apartment. Please come immediately with an ambulance." If you save a phone number of a stranger, you should absolutely state your address in the message.

This message will only be played if the other party confirms the call. If the first saved number is not reachable, every following number will be dialled until someone takes the call.

The goal is to get the service dog to trigger the emergency call if you are unconscious. It is a complex task which needs to be divided into separate chains of action.

Initially, you should train your dog to press the emergency button. Make sure that he can touch a certain point with his paw on command. To practice this, use target training to teach your dog to touch a Post-It note or the tip of a target stick with his paw. Form a fist around the treat. Then put the fist onto the floor and show the dog that there is a treat in your fist for a moment. Confirm any interest your dog shows in your fist with the clicker. Going a step further, you only confirm when your dog touches your hand with their paw to get the treat. After this, only confirm when they touch the Post-It note directly with their paw. Once they start to do this every time, you can introduce the cue, "good paw". After a few repetitions, add the command "paw"; you will see that your dog will readily put their paw onto the note, waiting for you to click. Now you can move the Post-It to the emergency phone chip and give your dog the command "paw". If your dog understands the command, they will put their paw onto the Post-It. Confirm as soon as his paw touches the chip. If your dog is still reluctant to place the paw onto the chip, go back one step and continue practicing the command using your hand.

Next, you should train your dog to push the emergency button with increasing force, making sure that the alarm is actually set off. To achieve this, delay confirmation more and more. Make the Post-It note smaller every time you practice until your dog doesn't need it anymore and pushes the chip upon hearing the cue "paw". If he now scratches next to the emergency button, but will not hit it anymore, you are moving too fast, and you should carry on training with the Post-It note for a few more days (before gradually phasing it out).

Next, designate a room for the emergency phone so that your dog can get used to finding it here. Practice the "paw" command a few times before, gradually moving away from the phone. Give the "paw" cue while standing about 19 inches away from the phone, then move away 40 inches more, and then 80 inches more, until you are in a different room and your dog has to walk away from you to reach the phone. If he has to open a door to reach the phone, help him by giving the "open door" command. After a few repetitions, upon giving the command "paw", he should open the door by himself to get into the living room. The last step is for your dog to push the emergency button – not when given the cue "paw", but by associating the emergency phone with an actual emergency. After all, you will not be able to give your dog the command "paw" in case you become unconscious. You need another person for this step. The telephone remains in the same location as before, and the two of you begin closeby. Only increase your distance to the phone after a few days of training. Simulate fainting by falling and lying motionless on the ground. Your dog will probably walk up to you now. However, when you are actually unconscious you won't be able to react. This is why it is important that you do not give in while the helper rewards the dog for trying to "wake you up". The helper should give the command "paw" immediately after. If your dog does not walk up to the phone right away, the other person can help him by walking part of the way with him, and by encouraging him. Many service dogs initially struggle to leave you behind when you are helpless. When your dog reaches the phone, fulfilling the command "paw", the helper clicks and rewards him immediately. Now you can reward your dog, too. Over the following weeks, make sure you increase the period of time after which you reward your dog; in case of an actual emergency, your dog will also have to wait until help arrives, so this encourages him to keep trying to assist you. Also, begin to incorporate other areas of the house for you to pretend to faint in such as the bathroom or in the hallway.

Once your dog is used to this, the helper should move further away from you to the door until he is invisible. The second person should give the commands from this location. He is hidden behind a door and should only enter the room after the dog has pushed the emergency button. Through repetition, your dog will build a link between walking to the telephone to fulfil the command "paw" and your "fainting". The helper enters the room shortly after the alarm signal sounds to praise and reward your dog extensively for a job well done.

Over time, you should delay the moment when the helper comes back by a few seconds at first, and then by minutes. Now that you have achieved your goal and your dog is prepared for a real emergency, you should regularly repeat this training at least once a month so that your dog does not forget how to behave in an emergency, even if if occurs eight years from now.

Nightmares (external task and cognitive behavior)

After a nightmare, your dog will turn on the lights upon command. Whenever you wake up from a nightmare, give your dog the command "light", and he will get up and switch on the bedroom light. This allows you to calm down and understand that it was a nightmare, not reality.

Indicating People Approaching from Behind (external task)

Many people suffering from PTSD are frightened of anyone approaching them unnoticed from behind, so your dog can signal people as they approach.

You will need a second person for this exercise. Begin by practicing in a quiet location such as the garden or a country lane so that you can train your dog under controlled conditions, and can influence how often somebody approaches from behind. Walk your dog on a lead along a country lane. The helper now comes closer from behind. When your dog turns around, click and confirm this. Next, you step aside with your dog so that the helper can get past, reaffirming your dog again for letting them pass. Alternatively, bring your dogs' favourite toy and play with him for a moment after he has moved aside. Click and give your dog a treat every time the other person comes closer from behind and your dog responds by turning around or a similar action. After a few weeks your dog, will start to automatically turn and look for the helping person when they walk behind you. Now it is time to introduce the indicating command. Train this following the same procedure as with the command "paw" for the emergency phone. Instead of directing the dog towards the emergency phone with the Post-It note or the target stick, you now point the stick at your leg. Give your dog the command "paw", clicking and rewarding him as soon as he scratches your leg with his paw. Gradually increase the distractions for your dog until he reliably responds to your command "paw" by scratching your leg (even when in public, surrounded by distractions). You are now ready to link the indicator command to the task. Give your dog the cue "paw" when the helper approaches from behind. If the dog shows the correct response, click, treat, reward and, after letting the person pass, a little bit of playtime. With sufficient training and repetitions, your dog will start linking the approaching person to the indicating command, and will start scratching your leg when the person comes closer.

You have to generalize this behavior and to apply it to other people. Reduce the amount of distractions, but use different people approaching from behind until you feel comfortable practicing this task in a residential area or a city centre. You have achieved your aim when your dog fulfils this task reliably and scratches your leg every time somebody is walking behind you. Make sure that there is never a situation where somebody walks behind you without giving your dog the paw command first.

Waking up (external task and regulating behavior)

Your dog wakes you up when you struggle to get up due to depressions or medication. During training for this task, your dog will learn to respond to a ringing alarm clock as his command. Set the alarm and hold the clock in your hand. Click and reward your dog when it rings. Put the alarm clock next to you after a few repetitions. If your dog listens up or walks to the the alarm clock when it rings, click and treat. Now place the alarm clock next to your bed and lie down in bed. Again, reaffirm any interest your dog shows in the ringing alarm clock. To train the dog to jump onto your bed and wake you up without using the alarm clock, encourage your dog to jump onto your bed using the command, "jump". If they react to "jump" by jumping on your bed, click and treat. Choose how you want your dog to wake you up so that you feel comfortable and motivated to get out of bed. If you do not want your dog to jump onto your bed, he can also stop in front of the bed. If you want him to wake you up by scratching your leg, practice the task "paw" as described previously, and then give your dog the command "paw" while you are in bed. Afterwards, link the alarm sound to both commands. Give your dog the commands "jump" and "paw" when the alarm goes off. If he fulfils both commands, click and reward. If you use an alarm to wake up in the mornings, link this task to your daily morning routine in addition to the training lessons. Give your dog the commands when the alarm goes off. Ideally, you should have a reclosable box containing treats next to your bed so that you can reward your dog as soon as he wakes you up. Thanks to the repetitions, your dog will begin to wake you up automatically when the alarm goes off after a few months or even weeks.

Finding Keys
(external task)

Your dog finds and brings you your keys when you have misplaced them. Prerequisite for this task is the ability to fetch. Practice fetching the key the same way that you practiced fetching medication. At a later stage, your dog will find and bring you your key by its sense of smell. Many dogs dislike the metallic smell of keys. You can make life easier for your dog by using a keychain made of a soft fabric, for example, which enables the dog to pick the key up more easily.

Start by differentiating smells. First, hold your key ring out to your dog and reaffirm every time your dog shows interest. If he sniffs it, click and treat. Place the key onto the floor. If the dog walks up to it and sniffs it, click and treat. Place other objects around the key. Ignore your dog sniffing any of the other objects and only click when he smells the key. Give your dog additional confirmation when he sniffs the key by saying "good key". Give your dog the command "get key". You are almost there if he finds the key amongst the other objects and brings it to you. Finally, you should place the key in different places like the floor, under the table behind the sofa, in a drawer or on a chest of drawers, during training. Keep moving away from the key so that your dog has to search several rooms in order to find the key.

How to create Distance (external task)

The dog jumps at you and prevents other people from coming close to you. Your dog's height creates a natural barrier so someone who is talking to you cannot come too close, slap on your back or give you a hug.

You need make sure that your dog learns that he is not allowed to jump at you all the time.

Otherwise you will send a message that to your dog that he can jump at everyone without waiting for a command.

First, train the service dog to react to your commands. Slap your chest slowly a few times. If your dog looks at your hand, click and give treats. Will they come closer to your hand? Do a click and give treats again. Will they try to jump at you? Encourage them to do so with a click and treats. You can now establish the verbal order, "please". If you say "please" often, choose another word to avoid confusion. Otherwise, your dog will jump at you every time you say "please". You slap on your chest, your dog jumps, you click, reward and say, "good please". After some repetition, you can shorten it to just "please". Once your dog gets the hang of this, he will jump at you with just the word, and not the slap. In the end you can add a helper and go in public to increase the amount of distractions. If the assistant comes to you and starts talking, give the command "please". Take care that you will confirm delayed in time so that your dog will stay at your shoulders with his front paws. You can now praise him for staying there for more than just a few seconds. From now on you can do this task in everyday life if you are talking to somebody and do not feel comfortable.

Bring Back Home, Or Go to the Car
(external task)

If you experience a dissociative fugue while on a walk, your dog will bring you back to your home or car.

At first, your dog learns the commands "home" and "car", and then how to lead you to each destination. You train every time you are outside together. Every time you go to the car with your dog, praise him and say, "good car". If you come from a walk and stand in front of the door, praise your dog and tell him "good home". Additionally, you could stand a few inches from the front door and then head for the door again. When you reach the door, click and say, "good home".

You could also head to your car in different settings. Be sure to click, give treats, and say the command "car". Your dog will always be able to find your car based on your scent. As you walk, you naturally lose skin particles that your dog can use as a trail to reconstruct where you have been. If your dog has problems finding your car in a parking lot, you can apply some liverwurst at the car door before you head for it. After some time, your dog should have enough motivation to find your car. Gradually increase the distance until your dog can bring you back to the front door of your home, or to the car door.

Your dog needs a few months of daily training until he fully understands this task.

Guide to A Safe Place (external task)

Your dog guides you to a quiet, safe place whenever you get a panic attack. If you want to get out of a crowd while panicked, your dog can guide you out of the crowd or bring you to a quieter side. You should start this task at home without any distractions.

Take a walk in the living room with the dog on a leash. When you reach a wall, click and give a treat. Say, "good side." After your dog begins to eagerly go to the side, you can shorten the command to "side". If your dog does not immediately go to the side of the room, you can employ a trick. Put a treat at the side of a room so that your dog can see it, and start the exercise again. The treat should be enough motivation to get your dog to understand what the command "side" means. When he begins to reliably move to the side upon hearing "side", you should start practicing in other rooms. After this, add more distractions and practice in public.

Guide to A Seat
(external task)

Your dog guides you to the nearest seat when you get panicked or do not feel comfortable.

You can start this task at home and go on with it in public later on. In the end, your dog should be able to advise you of any nearby sitting accommodation.

Take the dog and go straight to a bench. Hold a treat above the seat so your dog's head is right above the seat. In the moment that your dog's head meets the bench, click, give a treat and say, "good bench." Go away from the bench and start moving towards it again. Try to hold the treat closer to the seat so the dog's head rests on it. You should give your dog the "bench" command after a few repetitions. He will move closer to the bench on his own. Now you can train this exercise in different places under different sitting accommodations, and with more distractions.

Once your dog can reliably find a seat, you should add an at-rest command. That means you have to give the dog the "bench" command when there is no seat to be found. Your dog should now heed your call and go searching for a free seat. If the dog does not ignore this bench and moves straight ahead it, you need to correct him. Do not click and do not confirm him for showing this bench at this moment. Please do not do the at-rest command too often, so that your dog will not become frustrated.

For this training, you should find two benches next to each

other so that you can lead your dog to the next free seat, if the other one is taken.

Search A Room (external task and cognitive behavior)

If you suffer from hypervigilance, let the dog search the room for potential burglars. You need to practice this task in small incremental steps, which will be connected in the end.

First, you train the dog to search for and find a person. Afterwards, the dog learns to indicate this person, and in the last part, he searches an entire room and indicates if someone is there.

You need some helpers to do this task. You and your assistant are facing each other. Unleash your dog and confirm all of his interests in the person. If the dog looks at the assistant, click and give a treat. If the dog moves towards your assistant, click and treat. The dog ultimately has to realize that he should move towards the other person once you unleash him. You should start using the command "good find" after your dog reaches the assistant. After some more repetitions, you can shorten the order to "find", and your dog will move towards the assistant when you give the command and unleash him. It is time to increase the distance between you and the assistant. Your dog cannot see your assistant and has to run through different rooms to find you.

Stand at the front door and give the command to "find". Meanwhile, the assistant is hiding somewhere in the house. Follow your dog to confirm his behavior at the right moment. Later, you stay at the front door and wait for the dog to inform you whether there is another person in the house or not. Try to choose a new word that does not refer to flashbacks or dissociations. Otherwise, you could not be sure if your dog shows you that there is a person in your house, or that you are dissociated. Some are wishing that the dog barks when he finds a burglar. I can advise you against this by experience. After careful deliberation, no one should choose barking as an alert. How would you feel if your dog barks in the living room while you are standing at the front door, and you now know that there is a burglar? You want to have your dog next to you in this situation, don't you? It is appropriate to choose a command which tells your dog to come back to you to show you what is going on.

If you want your dog to nudge the back of your hand when there is a burglar in your house, you can train this just like other target-based tasks. Hold your back of the hand out to your dog, and give him a confirmation for showing interest in it. Now that you expect the dog to nudge your back of the hand, do a click and say "good nudge". You have nearly reached the finish of this exercise. After a few repetitions, you can shorten the command to "nudge". When your dog understands the meaning of "nudge", you have reached the first aim of this task. Practice this in different places, and with distractions. Does your dog nudges your back of hand every time reliably with distractions? Now you are ready to combine the command "find" with the command "nudge". Give the command "find" and walk with your dog. When the dog finds the assistant, do not click immediately, but rather say the command "nudge". If the dog nudges, click and praise with treats. Slowly increase your distance from the dog so he will eventually have to come back to you after finding someone to nudge your hand. Now you add an at-rest again, the same as the "bench" trick. There will be no person in the house, but you give the command "find". Your dog will come back to you after searching through all the rooms, but this time you don't give the command "nudge". You confirm him for coming back to and tell him to sit. From now on your dog will recognize that when he does not find anyone, he has to sit down. The next time you practice at-rests, you need to confirm your dog only after he comes back to you and sits down. If your dog wants to nudge your hand at the beginning, ignore him. Give him assistance by saying "sit" and give a treat.

The dog should not relate this task to only one person. It is important to train this task at different times with different assistants who hide everywhere in your house. Within 400 to 1,000 repetitions, and an equal number of at-rests, your dog will be able to reliably show you when an intruder is in your home.

You can apply this task every time you enter your front door. If the dog sits down, which will happen almost every time, you can enter your living room. If, however, the dog nudges your hand, you can quickly leave the house with him and get help.

Interrupting Flashbacks (external task and regulatory behavior)

By using a tactile stimulation such as "nudging", "scratching your leg" or "face licking", your dog can interrupt a flashback.

This exercise consists of two steps that are linked together. During the first part, you train the indicative command, which is subsequently related to the flashbacks in the second part. Before you start the task, it is necessary to decide which indication is supposed to be displayed by your dog. The command "paw" is trained the same way as indicating approaching persons. The command "nudge" is described in the section "Search a Room". If you want your dog to lick your face in case of a flashback, this can easily be achieved through reassurance tactics. Just spread a bit of cream cheese on your face, click and simultaneously reassure your dog with "good face" as he licks the cheese off. You will be happy to observe how quickly your dog understands the meaning of the command "face". Then, gradually reduce the cream cheese until your dog licks your face on the command "face" without you using cream cheese. Now simulate a flashback. Here, you will need a helper. Please note that a flashback is typically characterized by:

- Tunnel vision (staring straight ahead)
- Freezing paralysation
- No reaction

When you simulate tunnel vision. sit in a frozen position for a few seconds or minutes. Your helper will give your dog the "face" or "paw" or "nudge" command. If, in the beginning, your dog does not automatically achieve the command, your helper can guide your dog towards you. When your dog is executing the command correctly, click and reward. After a sufficient number of repetitions, your dog will automatically fulfill the exercise when you have a flashback. It is important that you also reward your dog after he reacts to a real flashback correctly. If you are not consistently reassuring your dog, the indication behavior will decline.

Calming Behaviour After A Flashback Or Panic Attack (external task, cognitive behavior, regulatory behavior and natural behavior)

Your dog is calming you after a flashback or a panic attack. Many people with disorders find it to be helpful and comforting to pet their dogs after they've experienced a flashback or a panic attack. Sit on the floor and motion for your dog to you, then click and reward. After this, you teach your dog to place his forepaws on your legs. To stimulate this behavior, click and reward every time he approaches with his paws. When your dog is standing with his two forepaws on your legs, you can use the words "good comfort" after clicking. After a few repetitions, use the command "comfort" before a click so that your dog automatically goes to comfort you. Slowly increase the duration of time your dog has to stay on your legs, and don't forget to reassure him. Vary the training locations from different chairs, couches, or beds. Exercise under increasing distractions. Additionally, you should give your dog the "comfort" command after every flashback or panic attack. After a sufficient number of repetitions, your dog will automatically approach you after a flashback or a panic attack on his own.

Reality Check (natural behavior)

Whether you see a shadow on the wall or think you hear something in your apartment, your dog can let you know if these things are real or not. This is useful to a lot of people and does not require much extra training because the dog's natural behavior is used. It is necessary to know how your dog reacts to strangers in your apartment. Will he approach them immediately, or will he only stand up to see who they are? Is your dog's ears erect? Is he barking? Using the dog's reaction as a clue, you can find out whether the shadows you see or the voices and sounds you hear are real. You have chosen a very stable dog who is not supposed to react on your moods, so if you see shadows or hear sounds, observe your dog's behavior. How is the dog reacting? If he is lying in a relaxed manner next to you, fast asleep, then you can be quite sure that the shadows and sounds are a result of your past trauma. If, on the other hand, your dog jumped up and is running towards the door, you can assume that the dog heard or saw something. In this case, it might be helpful to have a cell phone lying next to you to call for help. If it's not possible to call for help yourself, you can also send your dog to induce the alarm of your emergency phone. It can be useful to make an arrangement with a friend to call you on your cell phone after an alarm sounds. This way, your friend can find out what is causing the emergency. Was the alarm triggered because you lost consciousness, or some other event that requires immediate intervention?

Giving Public Support (external task)

Your dog stands very close to you in public locations. For example, at work or during a basic conversation. For this task, your dog must be able to execute the "stand" command from basic obedience training. Give your dog the "stand" command and hold him close to you so that he is touching your legs, either directly in front or nearby (whichever option you choose depends on whatever is most comforting for you). If the dog stays in the desired position after you command "stand", you can reassure, after a click, with "good stand closer" or "good stand across". You can gradually alter the command from "stand" to only "closer", or "across". Increase the level of distraction during training until your dog reliably reacts on your command "closer" or "across" appropriately.

Excuse from A Situation (cognitive behavior)

Due to your dog's behavior, you have an excuse to leave a certain situation.

A lot of people won't dare to leave a situation when they feel uncomfortable because don't want to appear rude. During this task, your dog learns to react on a subtle cue that is invisible to others. This cue allows you to say, "I think have to let my dog out." To fulfill the task, your dog needs to be able to execute the command "nudge", "paw" or "bark". In addition to the verbal command, you need to introduce a hand signal. As mentioned, the point of this task is that other people won't recognize that you are giving your dog a command. It wouldn't be very useful, for example, in a conversation with your boss, to suddenly give your dog the command "paw", so this must be done discreetly. At first, give the command while simultaneously using a hand gesture. After some repetition, however, gradually decrease the frequency of the verbal command so that your dog can learn to react only on the hand signal. Train under different conditions and with an increasing amount of distractions. Reward your dog every time he successfully executes the task.

Find the Exit from A Building (external task and regulatory behavior)

In case of a panic attack, your dog will lead you to the closest exit.

Begin in a setting that has a minimal amount of distractions. Starting from different rooms, lead your dog towards the front door. The moment you reach the door, click and say "good exit". After a few repetitions you should start using the "exit" command before you make your way towards the door. If the dog runs towards the door, click and reward. Additionally, you should include the task into your daily routine by saying "good exit" every time you leave with your dog through the front door. Increase the amount of distractions and start practicing in a public place. Start in a shop that you visit frequently, and use the same training structure that you've also applied at home. Practice in different shops until your dog can find the exit of each location on your command. When your dog leads you towards an exit, the leash should be slightly stretched. If, later on, you're in a panic or dissociative state, it might be helpful to actually feel that your dog is guiding you. It is difficult to feel guided safely if the leash hangs too loose. This is the reason why searching tasks such as looking for an exit, bank or safe place, are the only tasks where PTSD service dogs are supposed to pull on the leash.

Interrupt Dissociation (external task and regulatory behavior)

Your dog interrupts a dissociative state.

This task will be trained as well as the task to interrupt flashbacks. Several types of dogs have an innate gift to notice dissociations on their own and can alert them. Pay attention to whether your dog has this skill for you to promote and encourage. In most cases, these kinds of dogs will search for closeness, and will jump up on their owners, lay themselves down on them and sometimes show, while doing so, signs of stress like panting.

Follow a Person (external task)

Your dog follows a person on command when you are disassociated.

For this task, you need a second person. Give your assistant treats to hold. This person is supposed to show your dog that she is holding treats in her hand and then walk a couple of steps away. If your dog follows click and praise. Prolong the space your dog has to follow and say, after clicking, "follow". Next, increase the distractions until your dog also obeys your command to follow a stranger in public like in a grocery store or doctor's office. After that, take the treats out of scenario so that the dog learns to follow on command alone, not by smell.

Deterrence (external task)

Your dog barks on command when a stranger comes near.

This task is gladly used by almost all those with PTSD, mostly in the darkness. Since strangers can't tell the difference between a trained bark and a threatening bark, they can be scared by a big dog's bark.

It is not easy for every dog to bark on command. It is, however, possible to train your dog to barking on command through free shaping. If your dog barks, click and say "good speak" and give a treat. After sufficient repetition, your dog will come to understand that "speak" means "bark". If you have a dog who never barks, you must provoke him. Let someone else hold your dog while you wave his favorite toy directly in front of him without being able to reach. After a while, even the most patient dog will have to bark. You reward him immediately with a clicking sound, a treat and by saying "good speak".

In addition to the "speak" command, you can use a hand signal. The most common one is a quick opening and closing of the fist.

You will notice, when giving the command to speak, that your dog tries to form a barking sound that is similar to the warm-up vocal exercises of singers. In the beginning, your dog will sometimes only get a little "woof" out, followed by barking. If you closely listen, you will notice that your dog barks differently on the "speak"-command than, say, when the postman comes. Pay attention to dogs in television – trained barking on command sounds differently than normal barking. You will always reliably be able to recognize whether your dog is barking on command or because the parcel service is waiting at the door.

If your dog barks once or twice on command, you must absolutely make sure that he doesn't learn to bark constantly. Therefore, every time after you have clicked, you practice a termination word – "over". Your dog barks on command, you click, say "over". If your dog becomes quiet, treat and praise. After a while, you can just use a click on the "over" command without a treat.

Door Security (external task)

Your dog sits away from the door while you open it so that no

THE PTSD SERVICE DOG

one comes from behind unnoticed.

Your dog should be able to reliably sit before you attempt this. Attract your dog's attention with your hand so that he stands parallel to you while looking back. Give the command to sit. If your dog sits immediately with his eyes looking back, click and give a treat. After several repetitions, you can add a command to "look". Do this task whenever you are standing in front of a door. Most dogs need several weeks to get used to sitting with their backs turned when at a door. Increase the distraction with an additional assistant. If a person comes near, you should invite the dog to stand up by using the "up" command, just like your dog has learned since a puppy as a release command, as described in the book *From Puppy to Service Dog – Selection, Standards, Training*. If your dog stands up and moves after the command, click and reward. The aim of this task is for you to notice when your dog stands up while you are at the door. The assistant should attract your dog's attention after you gave the "up" command. Feeling tension on the leash is a good thing. Reward the tension of the leash with the clicking sound and a treat. Integrate situations into your training where no one comes along and your dog has to sit, as well as situations where someone comes close. After sufficient repetition, your dog will stand up automatically when someone comes from behind, putting tension on the leash so that you will notice.

Check Around Corners (external task and regulating behavior)

Your dog goes around a corner and alerts if a person is coming.

This task is divided in three parts: first, your dog learns that to recognize when a person appears from behind a corner. Second, the dog learns to alert it. Third, the dog learns to go ahead of you.

You need an assistant for this task. Find several sidewalks with corners that can conceal a person's approach. This occurs most often at side streets and crossings. With your dog on a leash, go along the sidewalk and ask the helper to walk the opposite direction from around the corner. When the person appears from behind the corner, click and reward your dog. Repeat until your dog shows a visible reaction, like pointed ears or a gentle pull when you go along corners, as if he is expecting someone to appear from the corner. Take a break so that the dog doesn't always expect a person to approach from around the corner, as this would be unrealistic. From then on, only click when your dog actively watches the corner. Slowly extend the amount of time between click and the approaching person so as to train your dog to have a long attention span. During this process, make sure that your dog really can hear the approach of that person.

After a short time, you will notice your dog has the same

behavior when there is a person behind a corner. At this point, you can practice letting your dog walk a few steps ahead. If your dog goes towards a corner, click and say "good forward". Train this way until your dog automatically goes few steps ahead of you to the corner. After that, apply the "forward" command first, which should be a signal for your dog to go a few steps ahead. If a person approaches your dog, the dog will avoid them or slow down. If there is no one approaching, the dog will go on normally.

Practice this task at a few different places with corners. After that, have several different assistants come around the corner. This will let your dog know that he should alert whenever anyone comes from around the corner, not just the same person.

You can also use this task "forward" to have your dog walk a few steps ahead in crowds or when you get off an elevator.

Disrupting Self-Harming Behaviour (external task, cognitive behavior and regulatory, corrective behavior)

Your dog distracts you from self-harming behavior through

auditory stimulation or a playful game. That way, you will be made aware of your behavior and will be able to refrain from it. However, your own actions and your contemplation are indispensable for this task. No dog can really keep you from hurting yourself if you yourself aren't ready to respond to your dog's attempts and refrain from that behavior. Your dog can only provide assistance; you have to accept and implement it yourself. A prerequisite for this task is the ability to fetch, as shown earlier.

This task is split into three parts. First, your dog learns to squeak a toy and retrieve it by command. After that, this exercise will be linked to self-harming behavior. Buy your dog a squeaky toy that he likes a lot. It can be any toy so long as it squeaks. Give the toy to your dog and encourage your dog to make the toy squeak. If the toy squeaks, click and say, "good squeaky", then give a treat and additional playtime. After a couple of repetitions, you can let the dog fetch the toy. Once he reliably brings the toy by command (for example, "get duck"), then you should always put the toy at a certain place – just like your medication and the water. Always stick to this command: First, "squeaky", and only then "get duck". Encourage your dog to make the toy squeak on the way over to you.

Now you can link the exercise with self-harming behavior. Simulate self-harming behavior. This is different for everybody, so act however you ordinarily act when you want to harm yourself. For example, if you usually harm yourself with a pair of scissors, take a pair of scissors in your hand and stare at it. Fixate on the object and appear absorbed by it. If you don't use any objects, it is a little bit harder to train your dog, but still possible. Try to be creative and link it to typical behavioral patterns, whatever they may be. When you fixate on the object, command your dog to "squeaky" and "get duck". By now, your dog should start running and return with the squeaky toy. When your dog reaches you, click, give a treat, put the scissors down and play exuberantly with your dog and his toy. Practice this task in different rooms – and also while seated, standing or lying down – until your dog automatically goes over to the toy and brings it to you when you pick up a pair of scissors.

Look Out
(external task and cognitive behavior)

Your dog gets up from down position and appears intimidating.

Service dogs aren't allowed to be trained as guard dogs and have to be friendly, but strangers don't know that your dog isn't really dangerous. A big dog standing up and posing will appear threatening to most people no matter what. Prerequisites for this task are the "down" and "stand" commands. Give your dog a "down" command, followed by "stand". If your dog stands, click, praise and treat. Slowly prolong the time in which your dog should remain standing until he keeps standing for several minutes. If your dog is having a hard time remaining in the standing position for a long, you can additionally practice by saying "stay". Practice these tasks in different places and slowly increase the distractions.

Guard Me (cognitive behavior)

Your dog can learn to jump forward and turn in the opposite direction to observe the surroundings. This task, just like the "look out" task, serves as an impressive deterrent. The friendly service dog is meant to look like a dangerous guard dog – even though he is far from it. In case someone comes close to you against your will, this task can help keep that person at a distance.

This task is practiced in three steps. First, your dog needs to learn to jump forward on command. After that, he needs to immediately stand still and pretend to scan the environment. Prerequisites for this task include the "stand exercise", and that your dog masters impulse control as well as the release word, "break". For this task, you will need an assistant. The assistant needs to stand in front of the dog with a ball, toy or treat. Make sure that you gave your dog the "break" command when starting this training. By now your dog should have good impulse control, and should have learned that he is not allowed to beg for a toy or treat. You have your dog on the leash while your assistant provokes the dog with the toy or the treat. Every interest your dog shows in the toy, you will reward with a click and a treat. As an additional reward, give the toy to your dog if he makes contact with you after the click. You should, however, ignore sounds your dog makes and not acknowledge them. You don't want your dog to forget impulse control, but rather that he learns to jump after the toy on command. Next, your assistant needs to hold the toy a little bit higher up. If your dog lifts his head to follow the toy with his eyes, you will acknowledge that action with a click and a treat. If your assistant encourages the dog, it won't take long until your dog will try to make a jump for the toy. In the very second your dog's forelegs leave the ground, you click and reward with a treat and the toy. You can start implementing a command for the jump – "good go". Over the course of the training, you can shorten the command to "go". Upon this command, your dog should jump towards the toy. Slowly try to reduce the use of the toy, so that your dog will jump forward on the leash on your command without it. Make sure your dog doesn't jump so too hard, as he might get hurt.

Onto the second part: how to get your dog to keep standing after jumping forward. For this, you give the "stand" command right after the command to "go!" Only click after your dog truly keeps standing upright. Lastly, you train your dog to pretend to be watching the environment. You will need an assistant again. The assistant will be standing in front of the dog, and holding a treat or toy as before, but this time horizontally. If your dog turns his head left to the assistant, click then reward. If he then looks right, click and treat. After several repeats, you can implement a command for this: "Good lookout!" After that, you only click when your dog turns his head left and right. After enough repetition, you can gradually reduce the work of the assistant so that your dog will perform the task on his own after you issue the commands "go", "stand", and "lookout".

About the Author

Lu Barrett is an Assistance Dog trainer and Assistance Dog partner. She shares her life with a Diabetic Alert Dog, and with a dual-function Service Dog who is still being trained. Her mobility is limited following an accident and she has suffered from type 1 diabetes since her youth. She has been training all types of Assistance Dogs and also trains on a volunteer basis for a non-profit Assistance Dog organization. Together with colleagues she brought the first Diabetic Alert Dogs to Germany, Switzerland and Austria and the first PTSD Service Dogs to Europe and is a member of the international working group for Diabetic Alert Dogs. She studied pedagogy and is an adult education lecturer, engaged in teaching others to train Assistance Dogs. Over the course of her career, she has tested over 5,000 pups and adult dogs and has trained with more than 400 Assistance Dog candidates. Lu Barrett is involved in national and international research into Assistance Dogs and has taken part in numerous studies on the same theme.

CPSIA information can be obtained
at www.ICGtesting.com
Printed in the USA
BVHW02s1508110418
513086BV00015B/197/P